QIGONG

QIGONG

Chinese Movement & Meditation for Health

by Danny Connor featuring Master Michael Tse

SAMUEL WEISER, INC.

York Beach, Maine

First American edition published in 1992 by
Samuel Weiser, Inc.
Box 612
York Beach, ME 03910

Library of Congress Cataloging-in-Publication Data

Connor, Danny.
    Qigong : Chinese movement & meditation for
health / by Danny Connor, Master Michael Tse
        p.   cm.
        1. Ch'i kung.   2. Health.   I. Tse, Michael. II. Title.
    RA781.8.C66   1992
    613.7 ' 1--dc20   92-1762
                                                         CIP

ISBN 0-87728-758-9
BJ

Cover photographs of Michael Tse copyright © 1992 Alan
Seabright.

Printed in the United States of America

The paper used in this publication meets the minimum require-
ments of the American National Standard for Permanence of
Paper for Printed Library Materials Z39.48-1984.

CONTENTS

ACKNOWLEDGMENTS

This book is the result of a number of elements which comprised a network of support, assistance, advice, comradeship and affection that were vital in ensuring the process came to completion.

Ip Chun (Hong Kong) who made the initial introduction
Tony Walsh, comrade and counsel
Joanna Connor for essential 'Qi' and patience
Alan Seabright for splendid photography
Moira Shawcross for typing skills
Patricia Bryan for collation
Dominique Shead for co-ordinating the process

Special thanks also to:
Patricia Cronshaw, Brian Seabright, John Hayes, Charlie Gidley, Norman (Nobby) Carr, Paul Sapin, Peter Kerrigan, Sue Johnson, Joel Thompson, Paul Coombes, Chris Thomas, Terry Ryan, Darryl Tam, Wes Wright and everyone who is part of the jigsaw.

INTRODUCTION

Qigong (pronounced chee-gong) translates as breathing exercise or 'energy skill' and has a long history in China. It has been recorded in medical literature since ancient times and is an important component of Traditional Chinese Medicine.

Qigong exercise includes different methods of practice, movement, postures and meditation. By adopting various postures of the body and regulating breathing and mind, a person can cultivate vital energy to cure illness and keep good health.

It is a theory of traditional Chinese medicine that vital energy, or Qi, has profound meaning. It is the material foundation of all movements of human life. When life stops, vital energy disappears. A strong vital energy gives good health and a weak one, poor health. Therefore, traditional Chinese medicine pays keen attention to cultivating vital energy to achieve good health.

In the *Medical Canon of The Yellow Emperor*, the oldest medical classic of ancient China published more than two thousand years ago, there is a chapter called 'Natural Truth in Ancient Times', which reads: 'When one is completely free of wishes or ambition, he will really get the genuine vital energy. When one concentrates his mind internally, how can disease attack him?'

How can Qigong exercise be used to cure disease and keep good health? The reason is that breathing exercise can increase vital energy to build vitality and prevent ill health.

Vital energy is the material foundation of the movement of life. It activates the physiological functions of the internal organs. In Chinese medical theory it plays the role of the moving power of life.

Vital energy is the essence of life. It promotes growth of the body and triggers the activity of the internal organs. The health of a person depends on his vital energy. An abundant vital energy establishes harmony among the internal organs, affording a sound mind and a healthy body. When a person's vital energy is damaged by congenital deficiency or postnatal factors, he will suffer from various diseases.

Traditionally, Qigong is known as a method of 'building vitality and warding off evils'. It builds up vital energy to cure diseases and keep good health. It is a self-training method of combining moving and stationary exercises. Externally, it strengthens the 'sinews, bones, muscles and skin'. Internally, it improves the 'semen, blood, vital energy and mental consciousness'.

Breathing exercise is a very effective measure to cure the effects of semen maladies. Correct and frequent practice will reinforce the semen of a person. It is effective against emission and other semen maladies of men, as well as gynaecological disease such as morbid leucorrhoea, uterine bleeding, or amenorrhoea.

A person who suffers from dyspepsia will benefit from breathing exercise, which improves the functions of his stomach, kidneys and spleen.

Briefly, Qigong exercise builds up the vital energy of a person and enables his internal organs to carry on normal and effective physiological activity.

Qigong exercise maintains the balance of health.

Traditional Chinese medicine regards the normal maintenance of life as the result of a balance of mind and body. An upset of the balance brings disease. Traditional Chinese doctors pay attention to such balance in studying the occurrence and development of disease, in pathology, in diagnosis and treatment. Qigong exercise keeps one's balance of mind and body.

When organisms exercise hyperfunction, a person loses his balance and falls ill. By practising breathing exercises in deep meditation, he can relieve his excited sympathetic nerve system and restore his balance.

Qigong exercise keeps the main and collateral channels in good order and regulates blood circulation.

The main and collateral channels serve to circulate blood, link internal organs, and send messages of disease for diagnosis. They are constituents of the human body, which carry messages of physiology, pathology and functions. When the network of channels exercise normal physiological functions, there is smooth circulation of the blood and vital energy, harmony among the internal organs, vigour of mind and physique. When pathological changes take place in the structure and functions, there is stasis in the circulation of blood and vital energy, discord among the internal organs, and failing health. Keeping the network of channels in good order, breathing exercise cures diseases and maintains good health.

It is also important to remember that parts of the body form an organic whole. A guideline of traditional Chinese medicine is to view the various parts of the human body as forming an organic whole. Either the theory of balance or that of channels verifies this conception. So does Qigong exercise.

While Qigong exercise deals with the internal causes of diseases, it pays attention to external causes too. In traditional Chinese medicine, the internal causes include happiness, anger, worry, longing, sorrow, fear, and terror. The external causes are draught, cold, heat, dampness, dryness, and fever.

Qigong exercise requires one to maintain a happy mood, but keep away from over-happiness, anger, worry, longing, sorrow, fear, and terror. Otherwise, the internal causes would take action, leading to diseases. Qigong exercise also requires one to pay attention to the external causes, to weather and diet. It advises people to take both fine and coarse food and a variety of grain, fruit, and vegetables.

Qigong exercise takes into account all parts of the human body and both internal and external causes of diseases. Therefore, it is a very effective measure to cure diseases and keep good health. That is why it has survived in China for thousands of years.

Michael Tse teaching

WHAT IS HEALTH?

How do you define health? The absence of disease along with a certain amount of aerobic fitness? This would reasonably satisfy most people. The Chinese view also embraces the possibility of a long life as being a test of good health. Long life is a part of Chinese alchemy.

Alchemy, which to many implies the transmutation of base metal into gold, meant much more to the Chinese. Their rulers of old, who employed alchemists, were not so much bothered with this chemistry, but rather with attempts to achieve immortality.

Traditional Chinese medicine follows certain principles and Qigong which is often termed 'breathing exercise' is the key to understanding and being able to be effective in your own health care.

The Chinese, for certain conditions, disdain exercises that exhaust the body, preferring instead those that nurture and create balance. Many people are familiar nowadays with Taijiquan (Tai Chi) which has become popular and quite rightly is respected as a beneficial exercise for health and self defence.

But there is an even greater jewel that has recently been introduced to the west. To compare the two is like comparing two precious stones, one cut in an emerald shape and one brilliant cut. Being of the same material and same weight, yet one reflects more light. Qigong, having more facets with regards health benefits has more curative methods than the Tai Chi exercises which are governed by their martial implications. Qigong, therefore, is free to explore the more healing possibilities of the human condition.

This book is an introduction to creating your own gentle health routine and enjoying the benefits.

WHY QIGONG?

Qigong is a most valuable part of China's medical legacy. Originally used for keeping fit only, it was later adopted also as a curative means and has proved its worth in both respects through long years of practice.

In ancient China a soldier came across a baby that had been left abandoned in a deserted village. The warrior was perplexed: he could not look after the child nor did he wish to leave it to the mercy of any animal which may come across it.

So he took the child to the town well. Climbing down the well he placed the child warmly wrapped on the stone floor at the bottom, figuring that if he could return or inform somebody then the baby's life might be saved. He held little hope of success, and left the village saddened, to return to his duties.

Thirty days later, war weary, he returned to the same deserted village with the purpose of giving the child a proper burial. To his shock and amazement he found the child was still alive. He couldn't believe his eyes. How had the child managed to survive with no food. There was some water in the almost empty well, but he still couldn't understood. He looked around the well and noticed there were many frogs 'croaking away'. He looked down and saw the baby blowing its cheeks and swallowing . . . trying to copy the frogs. By chance the child had been swallowing 'qi' (air) and this had nourished the baby through this period.

This story is told in Quigong legend, and the technique of 'swallowing the qi' forms part of Qigong practice, enabling the practitioner to gather more energy from air. This and many other methods form part of the rich plethora of techniques that comprise Qigong.

The wonderful effects of Qigong have yet to be fully explained in the light of modern science. Initial studies have amply shown how, with correct ways of breathing, Qigong helps to regulate the equilibrium in the higher nervous system and other systems of the human body, promote the normal functions of different organs and build up inner strength – all inducive to stronger resistance to diseases and to better health.

So far as the nervous system is concerned, Qigong helps to regulate the equilibrium between excitation and inhibition. For those who suffer from tension, practising Qigong will make them feel relaxed and will gradually improve their sleep. With respect to the respiratory system, Qigong can improve the function of the lungs and increase vital capacity. While the average person normally breathes seventeen or eighteen times per minute, one who persists in Qigong practice can breathe two or three times a minute during exercise without feeling out of breath.

Qigong aids blood circulation for the benefit of the heart. Different kinds of Qigong methods can be used to adjust blood pressure. Supplemented by other therapeutic methods, they can cure diseases like high blood pressure and arteriosclerosis.

Qigong exercises also produce obvious effects on the digestive system. Among other things, they promote digestion by stimulating the gastrointestinal movements and the secretion of digestive juice. That's why those who regularly practise Qigong usually have a good appetite and seldom suffer from constipation.

Qigong hastens metabolism in the human body, activates secretion in various glands, and helps to keep one's body weight at a normal level and stabilize one's frame of mind.

Students practising qigong in China

FROM NOTHING TO FIVE

In the beginning there was nothing.

Different schools of thought state this simple fact, although, 'who can understand nothing?' We need something to know what is nothing, from nothing comes one:

Everything has an energy field.
Thus we have the poles, North and South.

The energy field which draws matter to itself must have a centre where the two poles do not attract. The very centre. Thus we have the term 'centering', the state of not being unbalanced.

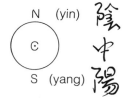

Meditation is in fact entering the state of being in the centre and not being drawn away.

As we are all a part of the universe. We have to understand the principle:

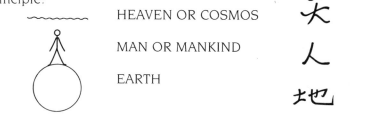

HEAVEN OR COSMOS

MAN OR MANKIND

EARTH

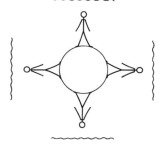

As we are attracted to heaven we are also attracted to Earth.
Man has to achieve a balance between the two.
Therefore within man there must be a centre which puts him in balance with the universe.
This centre is the key and the secret to many things not the least of them to be in good health.
This balanced diet together with balanced movement allows you to survive.

But we do not live as nature intended. Your life styles do not reflect this. This balance which incorporates good health also extends out in the universe where a balance exists.

The human being is influenced by two features: the weather and the place. We also are influenced by a technological society that imposes further stress on the individual.

So: As we have a North and South so we have an East and West.

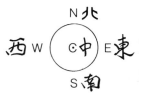

THE FOUR CORNERS OF THE EARTH

By knowing each direction we can find the centre:
But what is the centre.
This surely is the secret.
How about if the secret is nothing?
Having found the four directions and the centre we now have five points: 5 elements as we shall call them.

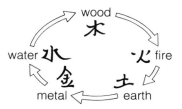

And may be termed:
WOOD   FIRE   EARTH   METAL   WATER
and they relate to each other in a continued process of creation and control.
We might say:
that water can dowse (put out) a fire
True:
but fire can boil water and change it to steam.
To give you an example:
No element is superior to all the others. Each interact with the other four elements differently and yet a balance is maintained in nature.
An invisible yet visible balance.
The ancient Chinese in their wisdom studied these points and further classified these elements.
Spontaneous exercise produces what is known as five animal play, movements that emerge from the body are classified in this way and thus we can find where in which organ the weakness lies.
Consequently the span allows you to observe your body and become aware of the condition and take steps to bring it into balance.

By bringing the body to a quiet state, your body will spontaneously move to adjust to your condition or illness, taking in positive energy and eliminating negative energy.

NB: For more information on the five elements, see page 80.

Left: *Dr Wu demonstrating Dragon Style Qigong*

Below: *The author, Danny Connnor, practising Dragon Style Qigong with Dr Wu of the Chengdu Physical Education Institute, Szechuan, China*

SKILL AND PHILOSOPHY

'Where did you learn it?' asked Nan Po.

'I learned it from the son of Writing the Assistant – for writing is no more than an aid,' came the reply. 'The son of Writing the Assistant learned it from the grandson of Repeated Recitation (which preceeded writing). The grandson of Repeated Recitation learned it from Clear Understanding who learned it from Whispering. Whispering learned it from Earnest Practice and Earnest Practice learned it from Joyful Singing. Joyful Singing learned it from Noumenon. Noumenon learned it from Penetration of Vacuity and Penetration of Vacuity learned it from Doubtful Beginning.'

'And what was it that you learned?' he further asked.

'How not to lean forward or backward' came the reply.

Qigong is composed of two Chinese characters, *qi* which means breath or energy (sometimes written as chi) and known as 'ki' in Japanese and *gong* which means skill.

Qigong then may be referred to as breathing skill, although Qigong nowadays is the collective term for a host of Chinese health skills that come from back in the mists of time, incorporating principles of Chinese health theory.

There are five major groupings of Qigong: buddist, confucianist, taoist, martial and medical. This book is concerned with the health benefits of Qigong practice which, in recent years, have received much attention in China. There Qigong is widely practised both as a health exercise and in clinics where it is taught to sufferers of chronic conditions and to post operative patients.

Simply, Qigong may be divided into two sections, active and passive. This balance of both elements of the human body, movement and stillness, is a basic requirement of good health making it possible for people of any age to practise.

The widespread growth of Qigong practice over the last decade attests to its appeal to the pragmatic Chinese who, like most of us, consider health and long life necessary for happiness.

Chuang Tzu and Hui Tzu were taking a leisurely stroll along the banks of the Hao River. Chuang Tzu said 'The white fish are swimming at ease. This is the happiness of the fish.'

'You are not a fish' said Hui Tzu, 'how do you know it is happiness?'

'You are not me' said Chuang Tzu, 'how do you know that I do not know the happiness of the fish?'

Hui Tzu said 'of course I do not know since I am not you, but you are not the fish and it is perfectly clear that you do not know the happiness of the fish.'

'Let's get to the bottom of this matter' said Chuang Tzu, 'when you asked me how I knew the happiness of the fish, you already knew that I knew the happiness of the fish but asked how. I knew it all along the river.'

What, then, is this ancient skill that, to date, has remained hidden from Western experience? Most people have witnessed Tai Chi, the early morning exercise practised in parks throughout China and south-east Asia. Indeed, for the uninitiated this might appear to be little different to certain methods of Qigong practice. Indeed, there are close connections.

Over a decade ago I visited China to study Tai Chi at the Beijing Physical Culture Institute. Catching an early morning taxi from the airport to the Institute I was able to witness the variety of morning exercises. I suppose I was somewhat discouraged to note that few seemed to be practising Tai Chi; people were out doing what seemed to be a variety of methods of early morning exercises such as stamping, shaking, self massage and standing in postures.

Briefly, Tai Chi is approximately 300 years old. It originated in the Chen village in northern China where it was taught as a martial art, a diluted version was then brought to Beijing and its popularity grew throughout the world and it became adopted as a health exercise.

No-one can deny the health benefits of regular morning exercise taken in the fresh air which promotes deep abdominal breathing and doesn't exhaust the body. The problem that Tai Chi has long laboured under has been the difficulty of remembering the movements and the length of time it takes to master the solo form. This has certainly been one of the drawbacks to its growth in the West.

However, Chinese wisdom and pragmatism eventually prevailed and a new method of exercise evolved called Tai Chi Qigong, com-

Kung-sun Ch'ou asked, 'May I venture to ask, sir, how you maintain an unperturbed mind and how Kao Tzu maintains an unperturbed mind. May I be told?' Mencius answered, 'Kao Tzu said, "What is not attained in words is not to be sought in the mind, and what is not attained in the mind is not to be sought in the vital force." It is all right to say that what is not attained in the mind is not to be sought in the vital force, but it is not all right to say that what is not attained in words is not to be sought in the mind. The will is the leader of the vital force, and the vital force pervades and animates the body. The will is the highest; the vital force comes next. Therefore I say, "Hold the will firm and never do violence to the vital force." '

Ch'ou said, 'You said that the will is the highest and that the vital force comes next. But you also say to hold the will firm and never to do violence to the vital force. Why?'

Mencius said, 'If the will is concentrated, the vital force [will follow it] and become active. If the vital force is concentrated, the will [will follow it] and become active. For instance, here is a case of a man falling or running. It is his vital force that is active, and yet it causes his mind to be active too.'

Ch'ou asked, 'May I venture to ask, sir, in what you are strong?'

Mencius replied, 'I understand words. And I am skillful in nourishing my strong, moving power.'

'May I ask what is meant by the strong, moving power?'

'It is difficult to describe. As power, it is exceedingly great and exceedingly strong. If nourished by uprightness and not injured, it will fill up all between heaven and earth. As power, it is accompanied by righteousness and the Way. Without them, it will be devoid of nourishment. It is produced by the accumulation of righteous deeds but is not obtained by incidental acts of righteousness. When one's conduct is not satisfactory to his own mind, then one will be devoid of nourishment. I therefore said that Kao Tzu never understood righteousness because he made it something external.'

prising eighteen simple-to-perform exercises that were based upon the movements of Tai Chi. These were widely accepted by the population at large, especially following their appearance on television.

From all over China people recorded the benefits gained from practice; illnesses that had been previously unresponsive to medical treatment were in retreat from this new/old exercise method. One woman claimed to have cured herself of cancer a number of times and along the way devised a simple method of Qigong practice that involves gentle walking and breathing. This is still regularly practised in the parks by huge numbers of seemingly old people. Perhaps the time may come when the parks in the West may be utilised in the same manner.

Qigong practice involves a host of different methods, meditation being one of the simplest. Many claims have been made and substantiated as to the benefits achieved. That is why it is important to balance such practice with movement, to release the collected energy that meditation accumulates.

YIN AND YANG AND ITS RELATIONSHIP TO QIGONG

The theory of Yin and Yang is the foundation stone of traditional Chinese medicine and is a central principle of the ancient way of preserving health.

The ancients found that the cosmos was an orderly, harmonious and systematic universe, and that everything in that universe was a unity of opposites: heaven and earth, movement and stillness, day and night, life and death, and so on. They divided all things in the universe into two major categories: Yin and Yang, which were also regarded as the two opposing aspects of everything.

Initially Yin and Yang were looked upon as something concrete. Later, with the development of man's thinking they became abstract concepts. Thus Yang represents anything that is superficial, energetic, positive, ascendant, rapid, intense, bright, open, out reaching, hot, etc, while Yin stands for everything that is innate, calm, slow, descendant, dark, contracting, closed, cold, etc.

Everything has its Yin and Yang aspect. Take a mountain for instance. Its Yang side faces the sun, and is bright and warm, while its Yin side is shady and cool. The human body too has its Yin and Yang parts, the former including the trunk, the back and the limbs, and the latter including the lower part of the body, the abdomen and the internal organs. Heat in the body is Yang, and cold is Yin. Sometimes the right half of the body is considered Yang and the left half Yin. Imbalance between the Yin and Yang in the body is said to result in illness.

Qi as a substance is also divided into Yin and Yang categories. Yin Qi in the natural world is heavy and tends to sink downward, while Yang Qi is light and tends to float upward. The purpose of Qigong exercises is to achieve a better balance of Yin and Yang, not only within the body but also between the body and the external world.

Yin and Yang are very closely related to each other. One cannot exist without the other although the two can be transformed into each other under certain circumstances. The two are completely different in nature and they tend to restrict each other. They are constantly changing and to maintain balance the rise of one is always attended by the fall of the other. It is through such an endless process of relative changes that things develop and life is maintained.

Based on the theory of balance between Yin and Yang, and in the light of the physiological features of the human body, Qigong exercises are composed of different kinds of movements and postures designed to improve one's physique. These movements may be solid or empty, dynamic or static, open or closed, and they may be performed during inhalation or exhalation – all according to the theory of Yin and Yang.

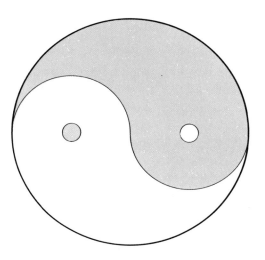

THE ORIGIN OF QI

The Chinese character for Qi is written two ways: (1) is the modern abbreviated Chinese version and (2) is the ancient method.

The character (3) which forms part of the whole means rice, shown in (4) as a rice plant with the stalk and root of the plant.

The upper part of the character comes from the diagram (6), which shows steam emitting from rice that is cooking in a pan on the fire.

The total composition of the character graduates through (7) and (8) and becomes (9) in its traditional form.

Michael Tse demonstrating 'qi' transmission

22

PRENATAL AND POSTNATAL QI

Prenatal 'qi' is the inheritance from our parents, which includes both strong and weak elements. Qigong practice helps to strengthen the prenatal weak elements (such as asthma).

Postnatal 'qi' refers to pathogenic elements that affect our health after we are born. Lack of exercise, a poor diet and exhaustion are among the factors that cause ill-health. Postnatal 'qi' is the first to benefit from qigong practice.

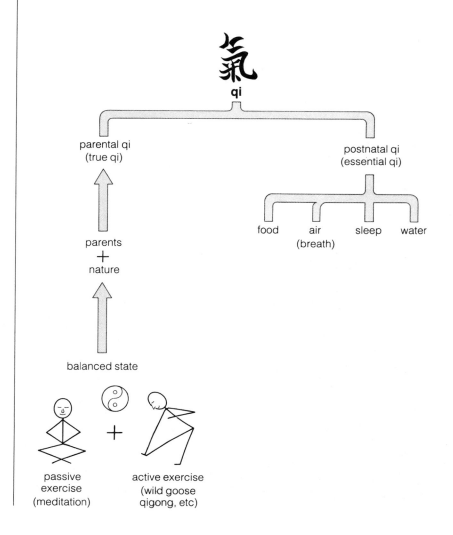

Major Acupoints On The Body

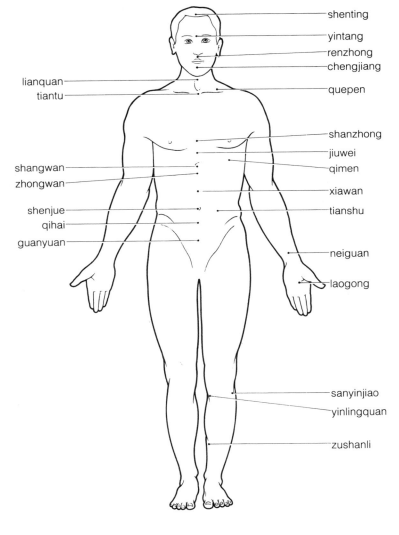

shenting

yintang

renzhong

chengjiang

lianquan

tiantu

quepen

shanzhong

jiuwei

shangwan

zhongwan

qimen

xiawan

shenjue

qihai

tianshu

guanyuan

neiguan

laogong

sanyinjiao

yinlingquan

zushanli

front view

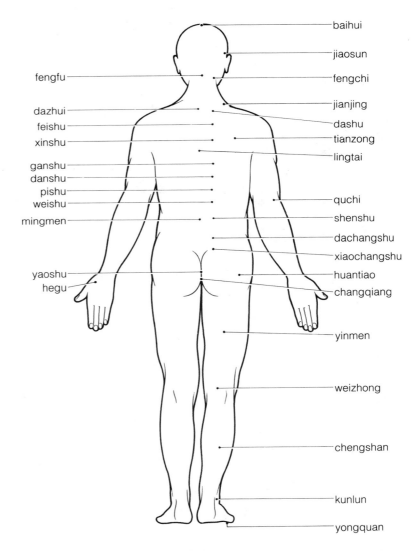

baihui

jiaosun

fengfu

fengchi

dazhui

jianjing

feishu

dashu

xinshu

tianzong

lingtai

ganshu

danshu

pishu

weishu

quchi

mingmen

shenshu

dachangshu

xiaochangshu

yaoshu

huantiao

hegu

changqiang

yinmen

weizhong

chengshan

kunlun

yongquan

back view

SELF MASSAGE

This method of exercise is said to calm the brain and stimulate the internal organs and is said to benefit the situation of those suffering from chronic disease such as insomnia, stomach and liver conditions, high blood pressure and heart disease.

Before beginning self massage techniques rub both hands together until you feel heat and then commence.

Self massage is very popular as a 'wake-up' exercise and is generally practised before postures, movement and meditation.

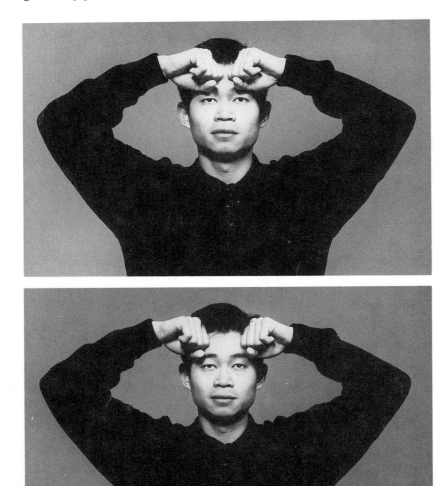

1 RUBBING THE FOREHEAD
Place both fists in the centre of the forehead, knuckles together, then gently slide the fist across the forehead towards the temple in a smoothing action, inside to out.
Cures: *Headaches, faintness*
Effect: *Opens the sky eye*

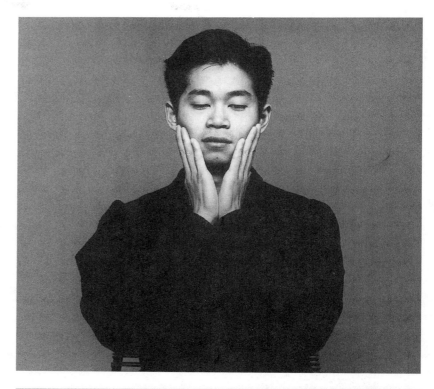

2 STROKING THE SIDES OF THE FACE UPWARDLY

Place the hands on the side of the face, palms inwards, with the finger tips just below the ear. Stroke the face with the hands in an upward motion.
Benefits: *The stomach channel*
Effect: *Improves the circulation of the face, helps waking*

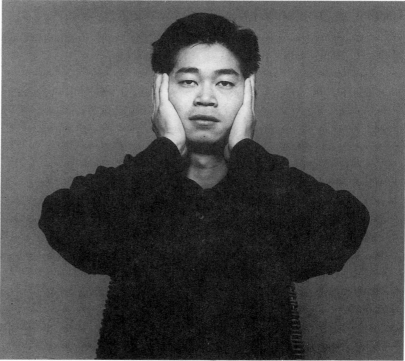

3 MASSAGING THE ORBIT

Place the index and middle fingers below the lower lid of the eye, starting at the inner corner. Gently rub the eyes in a circular direction. Repeat three times.

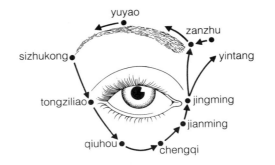

4 SOUNDING THE DRUM

Place the palm of the hands over the ears, covering the laogong point, with the fingers behind the head. Place the index finger across the middle finger, then slide the index finger off and back alongside into its natural position. Repeat six times.

Cures: *Tinitis, lack of concentration, tired body*
Affects: *Gall bladder*

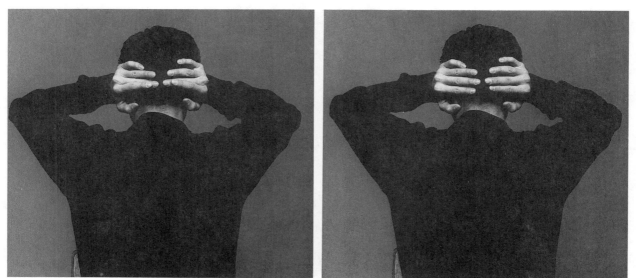

5 OPENING THE SINUS

Make a fist, then using both hands, place the first joint of the thumb on the bridge of the nose, then gently draw both fists away in a smooth action across each cheek.

Cures: *Hayfever, runny nose, blocked sinus*

Affects: *Large intestine channel*

6 WASHING THE MOUTH WITH QI

Purse the lips and draw in air. Hold the air at the back of the mouth and then push to the front of the mouth, without exhaling it. Swallow the saliva. Repeat ten times.

Cures: *Bad breath, increases the secretions of the body*

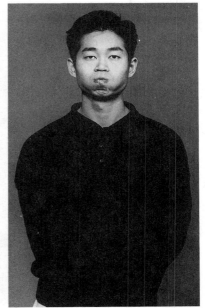

7 ROLLING THE ARMS WHILE STROKING THE NECK

Place the hands on the back of the neck, interlocking the fingers. Slide the hands from side to side. Repeat ten times.
Cures: *Stiff neck, shoulder aches, neurosis*
Affects: *Small intestine channel*

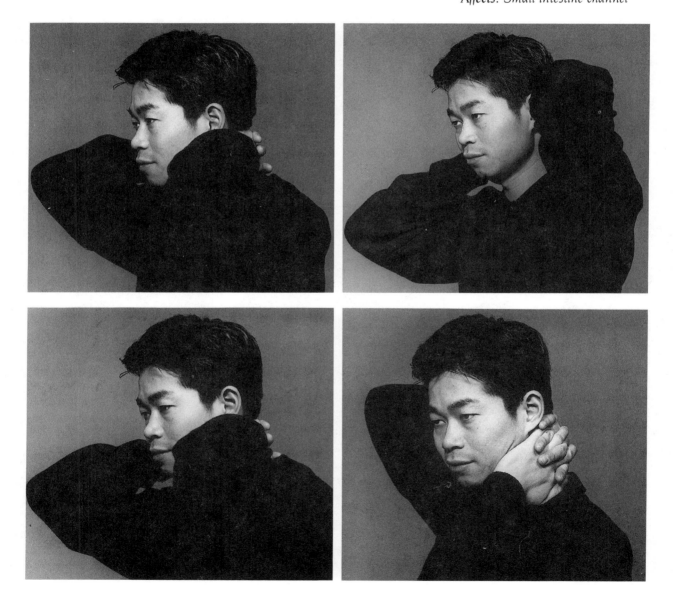

8 RELEASING CHEST PRESSURE EXERCISE

Place the right hand on the left side of the chest, at the same time taking the left hand behind and placing it on the back. Move the hands in a downward stroke finishing at the waist. Breathe out as you slide the hands down. Breathe slowly when the hands reach the finishing position.

Repeat three times each side. Men start the exercise on the left hand side, women on the right hand side.

Benefit: Stimulates the heart

Affects: Qi Hu point, energy gate, and Huang Men point on the back

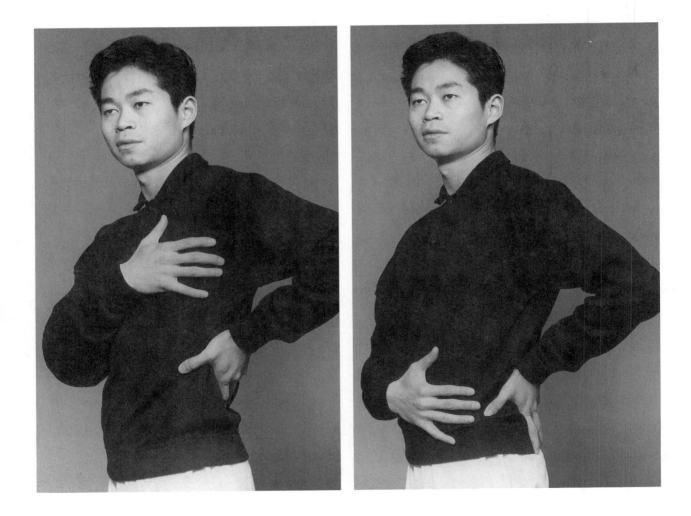

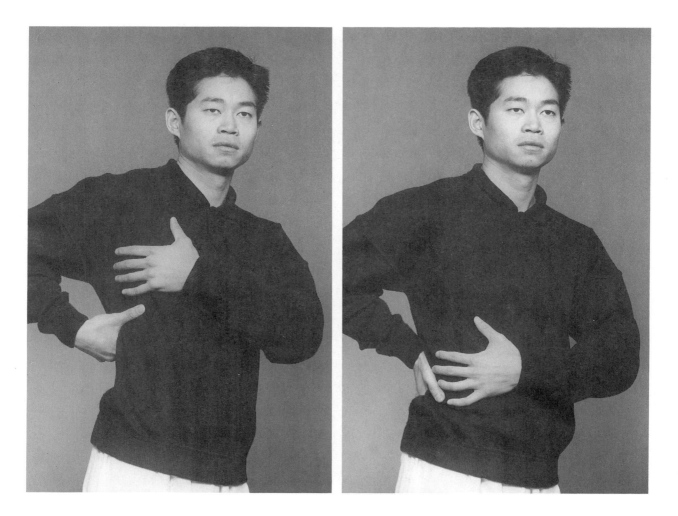

9 STROKING THE DANTIEN IN A CIRCULAR MOTION

Men, place the left hand under the right hand, placing them on the dantien (two inches below navel). Rotate the hands in small circles going from left to right, gradually making the circles larger, before decreasing to small again. Repeat twelve times.

Women, follow the same exercise but place the right hand under the left hand, and circle from right to left.

Cures: Stomach ache, nervous conditions

Affects: Collecting energy

10 STRENGTHEN KIDNEY EXERCISES

Standing up, lean forward and rub the lower back with the side of your fist. Alternate this with a downward stroking motion. Repeat ten times.

Cures: Backache, insomnia, tiredness

Affects: Shenshu, kidney point and urinary bladder channel

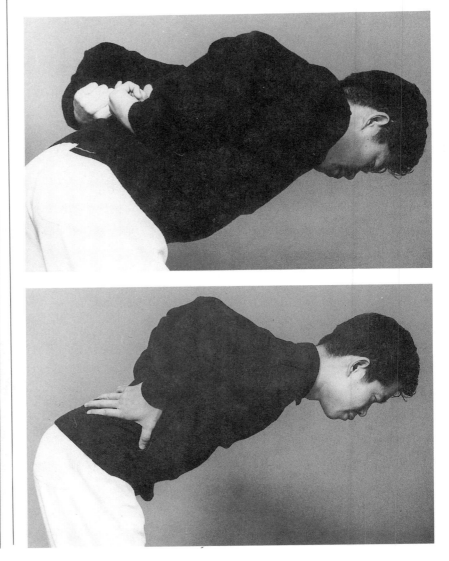

11 CIRCLING THE KNEES

Standing up, lean forward with your hands on your knees, and the knees bent slightly. Open and close the knees in an outward circling motion, then an inward circling motion. Repeat ten times in each direction.

Cures: *Arthritis of the knees and numbness of the legs*

Affects: *Liengqiu, stomach channel*

THE MOVEMENTS

HEALTHY WALKING EXERCISE (WIND BREATHING)

This exercise has received much acclaim in China over the past few years. Created by an old woman named Gup Lin, who is reputed to have cured herself of chronic illness through this method of practice.

When stepping forward remember to raise the toes to open the Yong-guan acupoint (located below the ball of the foot).

When practising remember to breathe in on two steps and breathe out on one, two in, one out. This method of walking also involves the arms swinging from side to side with one hand in front of the dantien on the completion of each step.

N.B. Patients suffering hypertension and heart disease should not follow the above breathing instructions. They should use natural breathing which is better for their condition.

FARMER LOOKS AT THE SKY

Stand naturally.

Put your hands on the kidney area — you will feel warm.

Hold that position for a while and then slowly bend backwards and look up at the sky.

Then come back to the original position.

Benefits: *Backache, tired body, bags underneath the eyes and the suffering from low energy.*

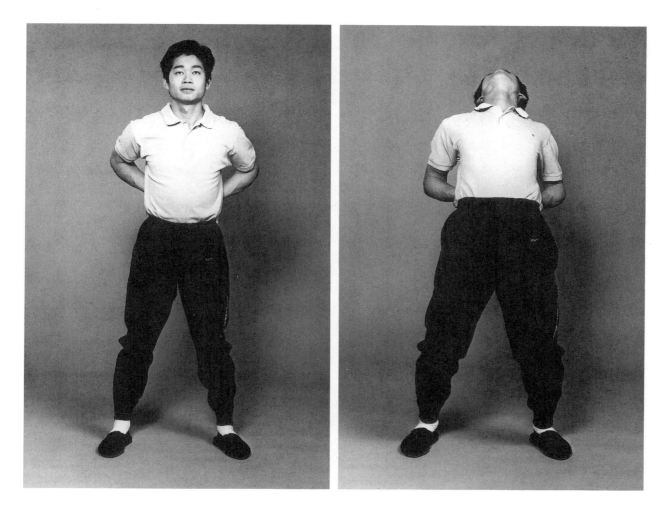

Tai Chi Qigong

Starting Position

Movement description: Stand naturally with the legs shoulder width apart. Close the mouth. Drop and relax the shoulders. Keep the hips straight and the gravity in the centre. Slowly raise the arms to shoulder height. Then, whilst lowering the body and bending the knees, bring the arms down, exhaling on the downward movement and inhaling on the upward.

Repeat the exercise six times.

Points to note: Before commencing the exercise it is advised to stand quietly in the standing posture for a few minutes in order to allow your body to relax. Keep the hips in a straight line with the body. Keep the head erect. Allow the elbows, wrists and fingers to bend naturally throughout the exercise. Let the arm movements follow the body in a coordinated manner.

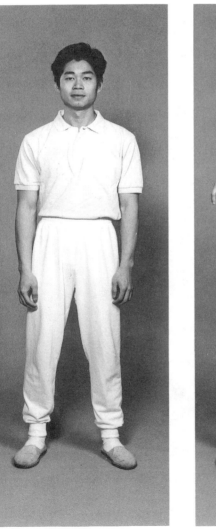

Health benefits: *This exercise is designed to balance the blood pressure and strengthen the heart. The gentle flexing movements of the shoulders, elbows, wrists, fingers and knees smooth the channels of energy and help prevent arthritis.*

SCOOPING THE SEA WHILE LOOKING AT THE SKY

Movement description: *Put the left leg forward, making the bow step. Lean your body forward, bringing both hands to cross in front of the knee. Breathe out at the same time.*

Cross the hands as they continue to follow the body as the gravity changes to the back leg. The hands open and separate, and the head finally looks at the sky as you breathe in. As the body changes to come forward, you breathe out and the hands gradually sink in front of your knee again.

Repeat the exercise with the opposite stance. Practise three to four times each way.

Points to note: *As your body leans forward, your back leg straightens as your front leg bends. Bend your body forward as much as you comfortably can. When looking at the sky extend your arms outward with slow natural breathing.*

Health benefits: *Practising this exercise induces the muscles to relax, improves the blood circulation and balances the blood pressure.*

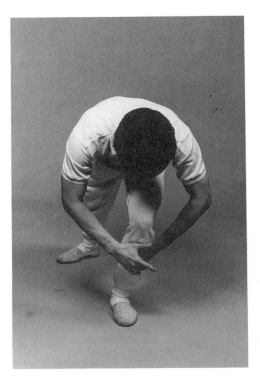

LOOKING AT THE MOON BY TURNING THE BODY

Movement description: Adopt a standing position with your arms at your side. Keeping your arms straight, turn your body to the left and swing both arms along a parallel path upwards and to the side, allowing your right elbow to bend naturally, left palm facing up, right palm facing down.

Repeat this movement both sides, and practise the exercise eight to ten times.

Points to note: As you wave your arms upward look up and behind to the open palm. Transfer the weight smoothly from side to side. Bend the legs as the arms reach the downward position in the central changing posture.

Health benefits: This exercise stimulates blood circulation and slims the waist and hips. It is also beneficial for those suffering from neurasthenia.

ROTATING WHEEL IN A CIRCLE

Movement description: *Stand naturally, bring both hands to cross in front of the stomach. Turn to the left side, keeping your arms straight. The arms follow the waist movement, moving upward around over the top of the head, palms facing forward. Breathe in at the same time. As the hand drops down the other side breathe out.*

Repeat the exercise four to ten times each side.

Repeat in the opposite direction.

Points to note: *While rotating the waist, the arms follow the movement and both palms face the same direction.*

Health benefits: *This exercise, practised slowly, is good for those suffering from low blood pressure. It also helps in the recovery of a tired body and reduces stiffness in the back.*

RAINBOW DANCE

Movement description: Raise up both hands to the front of the chest, straighten the legs and bring both hands over the head, straightening the arms. Palms should face each other; breathe in.

Move your weight to the right leg, bending the knees at the same time. Straighten the left leg and raise the heel off the floor so that only the sole and toes are touching the floor. Bring the left hand down to the horizontal level of the left side, with the palm facing upward. The right arm arches a semi-circle bringing the right palm over the head. As the whole body moves to the right side, breathe in.

Repeat the above exercise on the opposite side, swaying gently from side to side in a smooth continuous motion.

Perform the exercise six times.
Points to note: The hand movements should be coordinated with the breathing, and the movement should have a gentle and flowing appearance.
Health benefits: This exercise is designed to balance the blood pressure, aid the digestive system and relieve stomach ache.

OPENING THE CHEST

Movement description: Stand naturally, with your legs straight. Raise your hands to the front of your chest. Separate your arms to the side as you open your chest and breathe in. Bring the hands back to the body in a circling motion, finishing with the hands in front of the stomach, as you bend your legs and breathe out.

Points to note: When your hands are at chest height both body and legs straighten up at the same time. When the hands sink in front of your stomach your legs need to bend at the same time. Up and down, bend and straighten, breathe in, breathe out in coordination .

Health benefits: This exercise is beneficial for those suffering from depression, insomnia and hypertension.

NB: The complete 18 Tai Chi Qigong exercises may be found in *Tai Chi* by Danny Connor.

EIGHT SILK BROCADE EXERCISES (BADUANJIN)

The Chinese term for silk exercises is baduanjin, which literally means eight-section brocade. The four sets of exercises introduced here, each divided into eight movements, are more or less the same in principle but differ in degree of complexity. The first three sets are done in a standing position while the fourth and last is done sitting down.

To help with explanation, each movement of the first three sets is given a simple descriptive term.

SUPPORTING THE SKY WITH TWO HANDS

Stand to attention, look straight ahead and breathe through nose. Relax all joints and meditate for a few moments to gain concentration.
1. Slowly raise arms sideways, join hands over head, fingers interlocked, turn palms over and stretch up as though holding up the sky. At the same time lift heels off ground.
2. Lower arms and heels and return to preparation position.

Repeat exercise many times, breathe in when doing step 1; breathe out when doing step 2.
Health benefits: *This movement relaxes the muscles and stretches the arms, legs and torso. Accompanied by deep breathing, it affects the chest, abdomen and pelvis. It also helps to correct poor posture and keeps the shoulders and back straight.*

1. 兩手托天理三焦

DRAWING THE BOW TO THE LEFT AND RIGHT

Stand to attention.

1. Step to left and bend knees to assume a horse-riding position. Cross arms in front of chest, right arm outside, left arm inside. Then with thumb and forefinger of left hand extended and other three fingers curled, stretch left arm out to left, eyes following. At the same time clench right hand and stretch to right as though pulling a bow.

2. Return to preparation position.

3. Repeat step 1, but in opposite direction.

4. Return to preparation position.

   Repeat exercise many times. Breathe in when doing steps 1 and 3; breathe out when doing steps 2 and 4.

Health benefits: This movement concentrates on the chest area, but also affects shoulder and arm muscles. It helps blood circulation.

3. 調理脾胃須單舉

LIFTING ONE ARM

Stand straight, feet shoulder width apart, arms by side.

1. Raise right arm over head, palm up, fingers together and pointing to left; at the same time press left hand down, palm down, fingers together and pointing straight ahead.

2. Return to preparation position.

3. Repeat step 1, but with left arm over head.

4. Return to preparation position.

   Repeat exercise many times.

Breathe in when doing steps 1 and 3; breathe out when doing steps 2 and 4.

Health benefits: *Stretching arms, one up, the other down, affects the liver, gall bladder, spleen and stomach and strengthens the digestive system.*

LOOKING BACKWARD

Stand to attention, palms tightly touching thighs.

1. *Turn head to left slowly.*
2. *Return to preparation position.*
3. *Turn head to right slowly, following movement with eyes and looking back.*
4. *Return to preparation position.*
   Repeat exercise many times. Breathe in when doing steps 1 and 3; breathe out when doing steps 2 and 4.

Health benefits: *This movement involves turning the head, rolling the eyeballs and looking back as far as possible. It strengthens the neck muscles and also revitalizes the nervous system.*

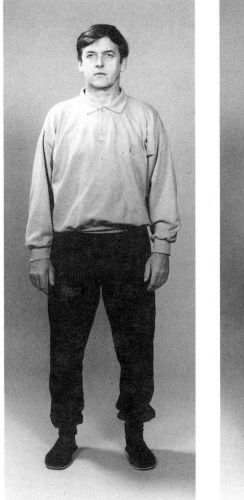

4.五勞七傷往後瞧

KILLING HEART FIRE BY ROTATING HEAD AND BODY

Bend knees to assume a horse-riding position with legs wide apart, place hands on thighs, thumbs pointing outward.

1. *Bend forward from waist and rotate body toward left; at same time sway buttocks toward right.*
2. *Return to preparation position.*
3. *Repeat step 1, but in opposite direction.*
4. *Return to preparation position.*
   Repeat exercise many times.
Breathe in when doing steps 1 and 3; breathe out when doing steps 2 and 4.

Health benefits: This movement involves using the whole body and is excellent relaxation.

5. 搖頭擺尾去心火

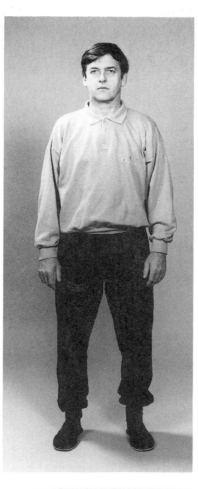

6. 背後七顛百病消

RAISING THE HEELS SEVEN TIMES

Stand naturally with your feet shoulder width apart.

1. Keeping both legs straight, raise the heels off the floor.

2. Let go and lower them to the ground.

3. Do this seven times in succession.

Slow down your breathing to remain natural.

Health benefits: *This exercise is said to be beneficial for the spine and the internal organs. The technique is also reputed to heal 100 illnesses.*

PUNCHING WITH TIGER EYES

Stand with legs wide apart, fists at waist and palms up. Bend knees to assume a horse-riding position.

1. *With palm down and glaring eyes following movement, stretch right fist slowly to right.*
2. *Return to preparation position.*
3. *Repeat step 1, but to left.*
4. *Return to preparation position.*
   Repeat exercise many times. Breathe out when doing steps 1 and 3; breathe in when doing steps 2 and 4.

Health benefits: *The emphasis here is on glaring eyes. Exercise with an angered expression is peculiarly Chinese and combined with fist thrusting helps concentration. This movement builds up energy and strength.*

HOLDING THE FEET WITH TWO HANDS

Stand to attention.

1. Keeping knees straight and head slightly raised, bend forward slowly and hold toes, or ankles for those who cannot reach toes.

2. Return to preparation position.

3. With hands holding waist, bend back slowly.

4. Return to preparation position.

Repeat exercise many times, breathing normally.

Health benefits: *This movement is especially good for the kidneys and waist. Bending forward and back stretches and strengthens the muscles in the waist and back, which in turn makes the kidneys and internal system firmer.*

NB: *This exercise is not for those with a clinical back condition.*

THREE STYLES

FOSTERING THE 'QI' IN A CIRCLE

Stand straight with both feet making a T-shape, rest your left hand on your waist and your right hand level with your dantien, palm upward, opening your thumb (which opens the Hegu point which connects to the large intestine channel). Extend the left hand outward, turning the waist slightly in the same direction.

Bring your arm in a circle upward (to face height) and then turn the hand inward drawing back the waist.

Bring the hand around and downward in front of the body to the Ren channel, at the same time slightly bending your legs, the hand returning to the position in front of the dantien. Then straighten your legs as you repeat the exercise.

From outside to inside fostering the "qi" in a circle, practise this exercise both right and left.
Benefits: *Tired body and low energy.*

FISHERMAN CASTS THE NET

Adopt a bow stance position with your feet, left leg bent.

Relax your wrists and swing your arms forward in front of your body, then changing the weight from front to back leg, circle both arms to the side of the waist, finally bringing both palms in front of the dantien, repeat the movement a number of times (practise the movement with the right foot forward).

Benefits: *Kidneys, legs and those suffering from arthritis.*

CRANE LIFTS UP ITS WINGS

Stand naturally with feet shoulder width apart.

Lift up the right leg, bring your thigh horizontal to the ground, leave your toes pointing downward.

Lift up both arms from the sides (like a birds wings) relaxing both wrists.

Bend your knees lowering your arms, let your palms press downward (repeat exercise) relax and you will find you will naturally breathe in on the upward movement.

Practise 5 to 10 times then change feet and practise using opposite stance.

Benefits: *Arthritis, anaemia and relaxing the brain.*

WILD GOOSE QIGONG

Dayan Qigong, literally meaning wild goose breathing exercise, is a set of exercises handed down through the ages among exclusive circles of the Taoist Kunlun school. Imitating the postures and movements of the wild goose, it consists of both vigorous and gentle movements in which motion is alternated with stillness. By stimulating a strong sensation of Qi, it provides an effective cure for diseases. The first 64 forms of the exercise take only five to ten minutes to complete, and are particularly suitable for mental workers of middle or old age. The movements, though rather numerous, are easy to learn, and may be practised either as a whole or part by part.

Dayan Qigong helps promote blood circulation and clear the jingmai, or the passages through which vital energy flows. It helps performers to take in health-giving air from nature and to discharge foul air from their body. It also enables them to quickly

Michael with Yang Mei Jun, aged 98, the inheritor of the Dayan Qigong system

master the art of emitting waiqi, out-flowing air, to cure diseases for themselves or for other people. It is particularly good for such ailments as hypertension and hypotension, heart diseases, neurasthenia, insomnia, functional disorder of autonomic nerves, gastrointestinal problems, rheumatoid arthritis and skin diseases. It also helps to take off fat from the obese. For the middle- and old-aged people, it serves as a kind of therapy for self-regulation and self-repair, one that benefits the human body as an organic whole. Unlike medical treatment, it has no side effects. Old people who practise the exercise for two or three months will find their muscles much more supple, joints in the waist, legs, shoulders and arms more flexible, cerebral functions improved and memory strengthened. Simply, Dayan Qigong helps to delay ageing and prolong life.

1 STARTING POSITION

Stand erect with feet parallel and shoulder width apart. Imagine you were propping up something with your head. Keep shoulders relaxed and arms hanging naturally at your sides, with palms turned inward, fingers naturally separated and slightly flexed. Close your mouth slightly and rest your tongue lightly on the hard palate. Look straight ahead.

Relax your whole body and remain calm and quiet. Keep your Qi down to the lower abdomen. Rid your mind of all distracting thoughts and stand quietly for a while.

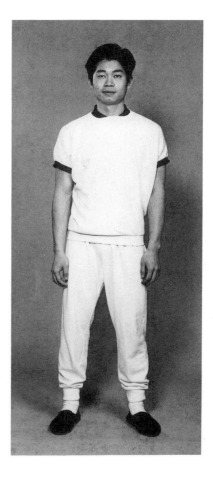

2 SPREAD WINGS

Raise both arms slowly to the front, with palms facing each other, until they come shoulder high. Then, as you go on raising arms, spread them out and rotate them so that palms face upwards, chest expanded, shoulders relaxed and elbows slightly bent. Meanwhile, bend body backward and lift heels slightly off floor with knees slightly flexed. Look up to the sky.

When you bend your body backward and look up to the sky, see that you do not overdo it lest you lose your balance or feel bad.

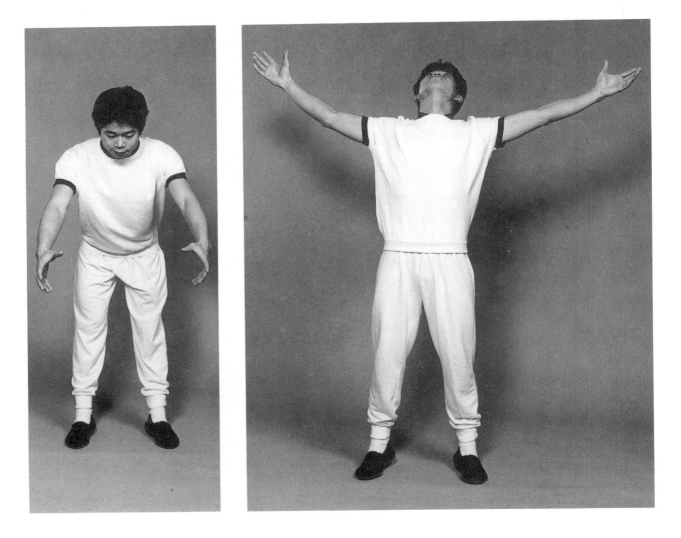

3 CLOSE WINGS

Rotate arms inward and bring hands down to the front of abdomen with arms rounded, palms turned inward, fingers of both hands pointing at each other, about ten cm apart, thumb and forefinger forming a curve.

As you bring your hands down to the front, restore body to erect position, draw in abdomen and set heels down on floor. Look down to the front.

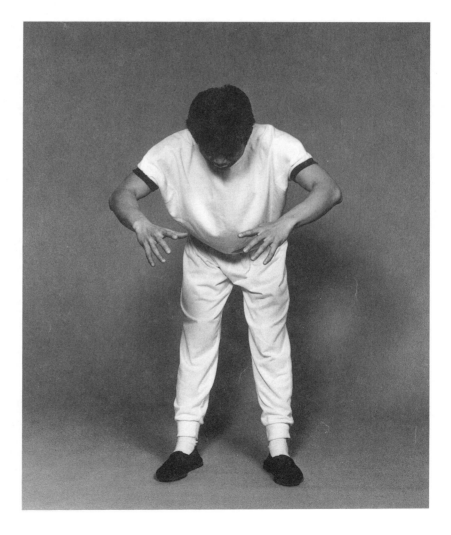

4 DRAW WINGS TO THE BACK

Lift both hands up to the chest, palms still facing inward. Rotate arms inward and turn palms so that they face each other, then consciously put forth strength and stretch arms forward while lifting heels off floor.

Rotate arms inward so as to turn hands back to back. Spread out arms vigorously and swing them down to the back of the hips with palms turned backward. Look straight ahead. Relax shoulders and keep armpits 'empty' (with enough space to hold an egg under arm). The heels are still off the floor.

5 JERK ARMS

Bend elbows and lift hands up to your back with palms turning up and fingers curling back in the form of a claw.

Rotating arms outward, bring your clawed hands up on your back and then suddenly out into the front for a backhand punch, elbows bent at 90°, fingers pointing to the front and palms facing upward and a bit inward. At the same time as you execute the backhand punch, quickly snap your upper arms against your sides and bring your heels down on floor. Look straight ahead.

6 DRAW WINGS TO THE BACK

Rotate arms inward as they extend forward with palms facing each other. Meanwhile, lift heels off floor and continue to rotate arms inward until hands are back to back. Then repeat movements as previously.

7 JERK ARMS

This is as before.

NB *The complete Dayan Qigong comprises 128 movements. The first 64 are for repairing postnatal conditions and the last 64 to repair prenatal conditions.*

MEDITATION

Meditation is found in the dictionary between Mediterranean and Midsection.

[A thinking over, contemplation from meditari to meditate]

i) The act of meditating; close or continued thought; the turning or revolving of a subject in the mind; serious contemplation; mental reflection.

(Websters New Twentieth Century Dictionary, unabridged, second edition-de luxe colour, 1982.)

Anyone reading the above can claim they practise meditation, and they would be correct at least in Western terms. Worrying would fit nicely into the above definition. There are two further definitions.

ii) Solemn reflections on sacred matters as a devotional act.
and

iii) A short literary theme treated meditively.

Section ii) is easiest described as prayer or meditation on the meaning behind religious mysteries. Section iii) is hopefully my attempt to extend this definition.

Firstly, everyone meditates! For what is lying on a beach (in the sun), other than meditation? It could be that's the real reason we come back refreshed from holidays.

Eastern thought on the subject varies. The Zen school seeks enlightenment; some Buddhist schools seek Nirvana: 'The state of perfect blessedness achieved by the extinction of individual existence and by the absorption of the soul into the supreme spirit, the extinction of all desires and passions.' The Buddhists claim that all suffering is due to desire and the ensuing disappointment due to unfulfilled desire.

Many people attempting meditation find that the mental recitation of a mantra (word) helps them to achieve a state of bliss. Thinking of one thing assists in forgetting 10,000 things. It's easier to let go of the one thing (after pouring the tea you can put down the tea pot). Meditation is practised and recommended by hundreds of doctors here in the UK and throughout the world, and there have been many medical papers written about its beneficial effects. Many people when practising meditation are at first unsure of how they should feel. We have to start as we are, we have no choice. There are various methods, though, and it's the technique that makes the difference!

The most ancient method of practising to relax is to imagine water flowing down the body. This is called Daoyin. Imagine water flowing down your head, down your neck, down your face, down your chest, arms, hands and waist, down your shoulders, and back through the hips and thighs, down the knees and shins, down through the ankles feet and toes, relaxing and letting go of tension. Visualising this process three times relaxes the body and allows the natural healing potential to take place. By the time you have repeated this method three times you will probably find your breathing has lowered to your stomach.

Meditation is not to get out of your head but rather to live within your body, which means that the external world has to diminish along with all its desires. Letting go, letting go, your house, your family, your friends, your job, your self, for when you practise meditation you are alone totally, you have no position, no power, no wealth, letting go of everything (as soon as any thought occurs let it dissolve) watch your mind searching for something to think about. . . Then let go. The mind is addicted to thoughts. I once read that the mind is like a giant chessboard and thought keeps jumping on different squares like a fly. Allow your mind to settle on your breathing, your body to relax deeper with each breath. Soon you will feel complete and comfortable, the fusion of mind and body. Afterwards you will feel refreshed. Rub your hands together and then rub your face. Regular practice morning and evening has benefits that are experiential.

Many people who have 'let go' of organised religion sometimes have a resistance to practising meditation because it resembles states of consciousness that they recall. But football is not basketball, it all depends on the technique and the employment. The old saying 'don't throw the baby out with the bath water' is a useful caution. I feel that many religions have appropriated meditation, which is natural to the human condition, and used it to control and indoctrinate.

In Qigong we advocate the use of meditation to heal the body, to allow the body's natural healing process to be released and at the same time to allow the balance that practice ensures to take place. This is the original purpose of meditation: to allow the mind and body to come to a state of conscious 'rest', and allow the body to 'heal itself' naturally.

Meditation also allows potential to develop and deeply suppressed abilities to come forth. It therefore can be described as a 'magical mystery tour' because you may not have realised your potential before, and you don't know how you will feel! Some people experience fear and alarm when they meditate and even visualise apparitions. This is described as 'reflecting on the internal organs'! Don't let this frighten you; if you feel frightened rub your face and blink your eyes. Often if you are tired the mind makes strange associations, and in such situations it may be better to practise meditation with your eyes half open. Everyone is different and everyone has a different potential.

Without 'self interest' there would be no venture into meditation. Achieving release from self interest is a maxim for success, but take it step by step, allowing yourself to let go, observe the happenings and reap the benefit of good health.

INDIVIDUAL POSTURES

1 SIMPLE STANDING

Stand upright naturally, raising the crown of the head. Close the mouth, relax the shoulders, think of the dantien (below the navel), half close your eyes (to avoid distractions). This exercise is good for insomnia, a tired body and is beneficial for those suffering from nervous conditions.

2 HOLDING THE QI IN THE DANTIEN

Stand, slightly bending the legs, hold both hands as shown in front of the dantien. Keep the mind on the dantien and whilst keeping the shoulders and chest relaxed let your stomach move when you breathe. This method of practice is good for the liver, kidney and stomach, ideal for those of a nervous condition, and those suffering from cold hands.

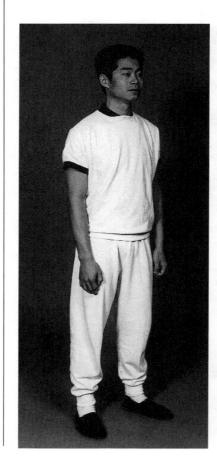

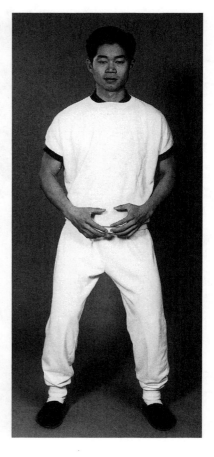

3 HOLDING THE TREE

Stand erect, with shoulders relaxed and legs slightly bent, creating a circle in front of the body with your arms. This posture is one of the oldest Qigong methods of practice handed down.

It strengthens the energy and is beneficial for the heart, lung and back.

4 SMALL CIRCLE STANDING POSITION

1. *Half opening your eyes, not focusing.*
2. *Bending your knees.*
3. *Concentrating at dantien.*
4. *Relaxing shoulders and elbows.*
5. *Straightening your back.*

Benefits: *Tired body, poor circulation, headache, kidneys and urinary bladder problems.*

MIXED STANDING POSTURES

After practising the individual standing postures, you may wish to attempt the sequence of mixed standing postures, which are invigorating and slightly more demanding.

Remember the rules: don't try to set records and let your arms move smoothly between each posture.

First, practise each of the mixed standing postures for 30 seconds, then change after two weeks practice – increase the time to one minute.

After three months you will be strong enough to hold each posture for two minutes, if possible practise in the fresh air, morning and evening.

Mixing standing postures develop the channels on the arms and legs. The twelve channels (meridians) benefit from this exercise.

1. Stand naturally, shoulders relaxed, arms hanging by the side of your body. Concentrate on the dantien and allow your breathing to deepen. Keep your mouth closed.
2. Slowly raise your arms to shoulder height; remember to keep your shoulders relaxed; open the space between thumb and forefinger.
3. Slowly turn the palms inward until they are facing each other. Allow your elbows to relax a little.

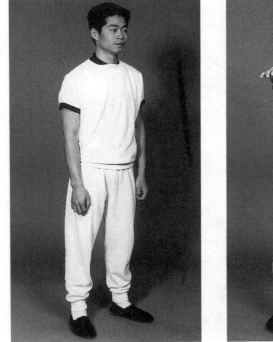

4. Draw both hands back in front of the chest, bending the elbows and keeping both forearms parallel with the floor.

5. Open your arms wide to both sides.

6. Finally, bring both arms frontward and downward to waist/hip height, remembering to keep the shoulders relaxed.

7. Resume starting position with the arms relaxed on both sides.

SITTING POSTURES

1 SITTING MEDITATION

Sit forward on the edge of the chair, straighten the back and lift up the head, close your mouth and put your tongue against the roof of your mouth. Place hands naturally on your thighs, this connects the 'Laogong' Acupoint in the hand to the Liengqiu point in the middle of the leg. Liengqiu point is the width of 4 fingers from the knee.

Draw the feet back until the toes are directly below the knee, this helps open the channels of energy through the legs, relax the chest and breathe with the abdomen.

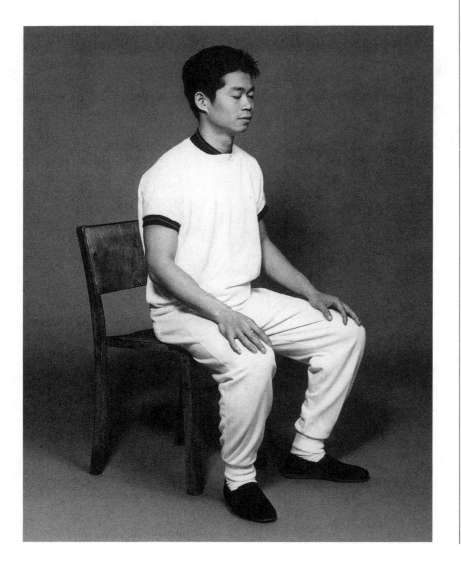

2 HOLDING THE 'QI' BALL IN FRONT OF THE 'DANTIEN'

Men are recommended to place the left hand inside the right hand and women the right hand inside the left, thumbs touching in both cases.

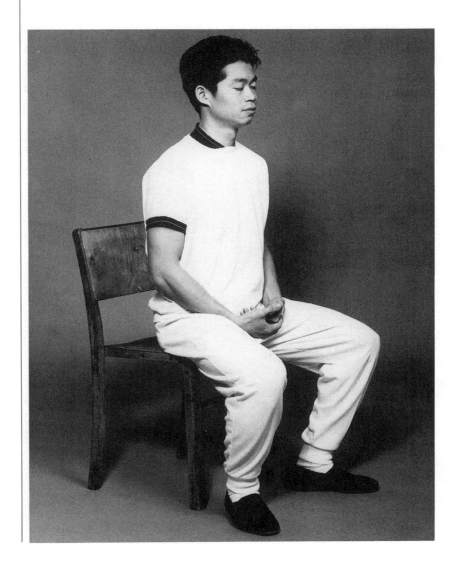

3 MEDITATION, HANDS FACING

Adopt the sitting posture and hold both palms facing each other, Laogong point to Laogong point. This method of practice will develop more energy and is best practised for developing energy.

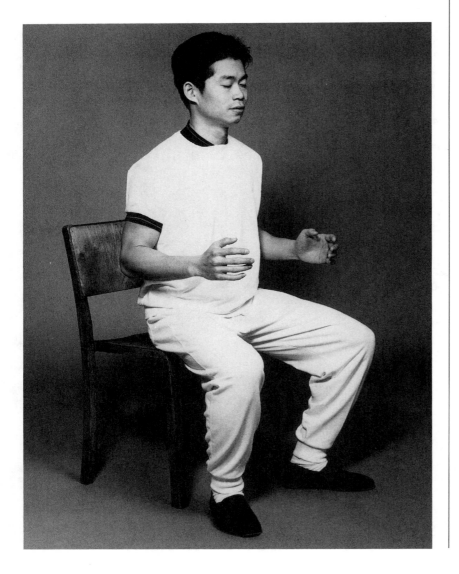

4 RELEASING NEGATIVE ENERGY WHILST MEDITATING

Observing the earlier postural points this time place both feet in line, the inverting of the feet allows the ankles to relax and the energy to flow through the Yong Guan point, located below the ball of the foot. To maintain the balance, alternate the position of the feet, this practice is ideal for people who work in sedentary occupations, this acupoint relates to the kidney channel and after practising for a few minutes the effect is refreshing.

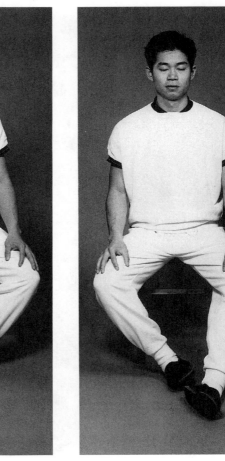

5 CHILD WORSHIPS THE BUDDHA

1. *Laogong point to Laogong point.*
2. *Concentrating at dantien.*
3. *Relax the shoulders and elbows.*
4. *Sitting at the edge of chair.*
5. *Do not sit back.*

Benefits: *Heart attack, cold hands, poor circulation.*

6 BUDDHA DOES MEDITATION

1. *Sitting on a chair or lotus sitting (crossed legs).*
2. *Closing the thumb and index fingers.*
3. *Left palm facing upward.*
4. *Right palm facing downward.*
5. *Sitting at the edge of the chair.*
6. *Closing eyes.*
Benefits: *Stomach and liver problems, poor circulation.*

Michael meditating

THE FIVE ELEMENTS

Bear

The five elements are understood better as forces, powers and agents rather than as material elements.

The emphasis is on principles and laws of operation. The outlook is dynamic and not static. In point of process there is contradiction as well as harmony and in point of reality there is unity in multiplicity.

Each of the five elements has its special associations, ranging from particular organs in the human body, colours, flavours, emotions, etc, as shown below:

	Water	Wood	Fire	Earth	Metal
ORGANS	kidneys	liver	heart	spleen	lungs
ANIMAL	bear	deer	bird	monkey	tiger
COLOUR	blue/black	green	red	yellow	white
SOUND	groaning	shouting	laughing	singing	weeping
SMELL	putrid	fancid	scorched	fragrant	rotten
TASTE	salty	sour	bitter	sweet	pungent
EMOTION	fear	anger	joy	sympathy	grief
SEASON	winter	spring	summer	late summer	autumn
TIME OF DAY	3-7pm	11pm-1am	11am-3pm 7-11pm	7-11am	3-7am

Deer

FIVE ELEMENT SPONTANEOUS EXERCISE THERAPY

Yawning, scratching, rubbing, stretching, groaning, even crying – all these activities bring your body to a more comfortable state. The practice of Spontaneous Qigong gives your body the opportunity to bring itself to a balanced state. Qigong theory recognises that the internal and the external are connected. Energy flowing through the internal organs (given the opportunity) will express itself through an external posture or movement. Movements such as neck twisting, face rubbing, in fact all movements that we practise involuntarily, can be said to have behind them a qigong theory based on acupuncture channels.

Bird

Monkey

Tiger

Spontaneous qigong is interwoven with five element theory (shown opposite) and the movements shown are the type of movements that have been connected to different organs; the bear posture is very useful for those with stiffness in the kidney area. Just stand up, relax, close your eyes, bend over to a comfortable position and see if you feel comfortable. Stay there if it feels good! The whole purpose of spontaneous qigong is to relax and feel your condition. Practice is very refreshing and by allowing spontaneous movement to happen causes the effect of unravelling tension which has found its way into the body tissue.

The bird posture which stimulates the heart channel allows an opening of the back and a reduction of pressure on the chest.

The tiger posture (all the animal depictions are part of this ancient legacy) relates to the lung. There may be the desire to make sounds – coughing for example has a metallic rasp that helps clear the lung passages. Raising your arms above your head, stretching, representing a deer, is said to be beneficial to the spleen.

Gentle guidance is recommended in the begining as some people may feel dizzy or unwell. Those suffering from hypotension should practise with their eyes half-closed to avoid fainting. A few guided sessions are all that is required to learn how to benefit from this unique method of relaxation. Those who practise meditation should practise spontaneous qigong before meditation.

First you must release negative energy then gather positive energy – the balance of yin and yang.

Of course, there are a multiplicity of movements that a person could make. Ideally they should find the movements that suit their 'individual' condition. Don't worry if you thought of doing a movement or if your body spontaneously began moving in a certain manner on its own. Sometimes the body may shake or convulse. Not letting jerking movements take over the body too much is another reason why a guide is important for the first few attempts.

Relaxing music helps the mind to relax and allows the body to enter into itself. If you have practised taichi or yoga or dance you may find your body during a spontaneous qigong session performing some of these movements, or you may even find yourself standing still. People often remark after one hours practice that it felt like only twenty minutes! Reports the following day of sound sleep (for some people almost an impossibility) show that the practice of spontaneous qigong allows the body to achieve a state of balance.

The term 'moving meditation' has been used to describe spontaneous qigong; the Greeks had a word for it: kinesiatrics or 'healing through movement'. Unblocking the channels of energy in the body allow the clear flow of 'qi' (energy) that is a pre-requisite for good health, according to Traditional Chinese Medicine.

QUESTIONS AND ANSWERS ON QIGONG PRACTICE

Danny Connor: Before we talk about Qigong, tell us how you first became involved in this study of Chinese skills.

Michael Tse: When I was aged about fifteen living in Hong Kong I broke my arm whilst playing, and my father took me to see his brother who was a herbalist and bonesetter. I had to visit him regularly. On one of my visits I saw him practising a martial art with some people; up to that point I didn't know he knew these skills. At that time Hong Kong was gripped with 'Kung Fu fever' because of the Bruce Lee phenomenon. I begged him to teach me, but he told me I must get permission from my father and furthermore that I must not use it for fighting. After meeting with my father he accepted me. The style he began to teach me was Wing Chun. He told me that I would have to help him collect herbs in the country-side and help him pound and prepare the herbs. Many people would come with various ailments and injuries. I had to mix, shred and help prepare these concoctions. I also saw him practise some exercises that didn't seem to have a martial application, but my interest was all-enveloping and I wanted to learn as much as possible.

DC: Beside the Wing Chun, you saw him practising some other exercise, which wasn't a martial art?

MT: He didn't say what it was, but I had heard him mention Qigong sometimes, so I started to think, about what it was. But when I was younger, I heard about Qigong more just as a supplementary exercise to Kung Fu.

DC: Was Qigong traditionally secret?

MT: Yes. Qigong is basically very traditional, and used to include superstitious thought, which has since been discarded, because I think a long time ago people didn't understand the method of how to balance their relation with nature. So we used a lot of methods. If a teacher didn't explain things, you thought it was something religious, but a good teacher would explain that we were doing something with nature, with the breathing, with the movement, with the mind. So Qigong basically combines the elements: one is breathing, one is movement or posture and the other is the mind.

DC: I see. So the purpose of Qigong is to be in tune with nature?

MT: Yes. I think that first of all we have to understand why we do

Michael Tse and Danny Connor researching Tai Chi Qigong *techniques*

Qigong, what it is. Actually I would say that everybody is already doing Qigong in one form or another, but just giving it a name – animals, all living things, plants, flowers, they find the way to survive on the earth. So the way to survive is with nature, and that is Qigong skill.

DC: So that means that sneezing or yawning is also Qigong?

MT: Exactly! In the morning, if we stretch, we do it because we haven't moved our body for a couple of hours, so when we wake up and open our eyes, we need to stretch. When our eyes are itching, we will put our hands to our eyes. It is a kind of reaction with nature, with part of our body.

DC: You mentioned the word 'balance' earlier. What you were talking about were movements to bring the body to a state of balance.

MT: That's the point, yes. To bring the body into balance, with balance following nature naturally.

DC: In the West, people have known of acupuncture for the past thirty years or so. How does Qigong relate to acupuncture?

MT: First we have to find out which came first. Basically, Qigong appeared earlier than acupuncture. For example when people have a stomach ache, they automatically put their hands on their stomach. When people have a headache, they will put a hand on their head. When people have a back problem, they will automatically slap their back. When a particular area of the body is stimulated, it brings relief as each area of the body relates to our channels and organs. That part remembers it, we try to record it and eventually this area, this part will relate to our internal organs. So eventually we find in these channels an acupuncture point. But when we are slapping, holding or moving the body, rubbing, this movement is like the exercise of Qigong, stimulating the channel and the acupuncture point. So that's why, when we do the exercise or connect with the channels and acupuncture points, we bring about a state of balance. Yoga for example has lots of methods that relate to health, but these are different from Qigong because they haven't got all the acupuncture points and channels behind them.

DC: Many people are aware of the Chinese practising early morning exercise. In China I've seen many people doing various exercises, slapping, stroking, jumping, even shouting. How widely practised is Qigong in China?

MT: Oh, I can say that everywhere in China, especially in big cities, every morning you can see loads of people gathered together in the park to practise exercises. Some follow the intructor and some come together to practise the form or movement, because, for the Chinese, health and long life are always concerns to be emphasised. That's why old people, when they retire or when they have a problem, go out in the morning and practise some simple exercises. This keeps them healthy and stronger and keeps their minds clear.

DC: Is Qigong now widely used in hospitals in China?

MT: Yes, I would say most of the hospitals in China now provide Qigong therapy especially in traditional Chinese medicine centres. In a way, patients receive a lot of help from Qigong practise and consequently people need to take less medicine and recover quicker. People are more interested in helping themselves. Because a lot of people in the West rely on medicine so much, they miss the connection with the human condition and the healing possibilities that they have.

DC: You are saying that people, through various Qigong practises, can reduce the amount of medicine they may need to take?

MT: Yes, and also because of Qigong practice we can recover energy quicker. Look at the difference between young and old people – old people get illnesses quicker because in young people the energy is still strong: when they have a problem or injury, they can recover quicker. They don't need to tell their parents they have a problem; they can recover in a couple of days. But for older people, one illness can cause another because the energy is not strong enough and causes lack of resistance to illness.

DC: Young people nowadays practise disco dancing. Would you view disco dancing as a form of Qigong in terms of why young people are healthy?

MT: In Western dancing you move the body, but sometimes you keep moving the body, and people lose the rhythm of breathing and movement, the fast and slow movement together, and so it causes you to use a lot of energy. When you've finished dancing, you will breathe hard, exhausted even because you are using up energy. It is like people who do a lot of physical training – they finish exhausted. But if you catch the right rhythm, get the balance, move the right side and the left side together, using the centre, your waist, your back, when you finish your energy will still be strong and your body will not be exhausted. That is the difference between the Western exercise and the Eastern exercise.

DC: Since you came to the West and saw people, do you think people in the West take enough exercise?

MT: No, I don't think so. Not just in the West, but even in China and the East, most people living in the city don't take enough exercise.

DC: Do you think that people, because they don't practise any exercise, look older than their years?

MT: I can't tell the difference between the West and East, but definitely if people don't take enough exercise they will get tired easily and consequently catch simple illnesses. A lot of people, whether in the West or East, do sport, but sport sometimes uses too much energy. They also damage their joints or hurt their back. China has a long history of Qigong, even people living in the city are still concerned about health, and when they have an early morning break they will go to practise and after work they will do some simple exercise. So it is like maintaining a car.

DC: In the book are shown self massage and various exercises and meditation. What was the purpose of choosing these exercises to illustrate this introduction to Qigong?

MT: This was because they are for the beginner – I think these exercises are very useful for people starting to do Qigong. First we do some self-massaging, rubbing the body to stimulate some of the acupuncture points and channels, remembering to keep the body warm before we start to do the exercises. It is no good doing exercises straightaway before we relax. After relaxation we do simple gentle exercises, smoothing the channels, developing the energy, gathering the energy from nature and afterwards meditation. It is like Yin and Yang. After movement, Yang, we gather Yin, for collecting the energy to the centre. This is the basic technique for all people.

DC: So massage, exercise and meditation, in that order, are recommended. Are there any people, in any condition, for whom Qigong is not recommended?

MT: Everybody can practise the exercises shown in the book. Some people, maybe if they are pregnant should refrain from exertion.

DC: So more or less all ages, all conditions, can practise safely. Having attended many of your lectures, Michael, I think one point may be interesting and that is, if a woman is menstruating, then you mention that it is not recommended for her to meditate on the dantien.

MT: Actually it doesn't matter. A woman with a period can still concentrate her mind on the dantien. But just in case, if some women have heavy periods, I suggest they concentrate on sanjung an area in the middle of the chest. But normally it should be alright.

DC: What improved conditions have you seen in people who practise Qigong?

MT: The first thing I see is that they begin to look younger and then secondly I see they start to look beautiful. Thirdly I see they begin to look stronger, because when we get older we lose a lot of energy. You can see the spirit on the face of some people, even if they are old. If you look at some young people, especially if they've had a very hard life, they can still look older than their years. So it depends on the energy. People look pretty because the energy comes to their face, the eyes become strong, and the skin soft because the internal organs become stronger. Soon they begin to glow with health.

DC: Is this because their bodies come into a state of balance?

MT: Yes, a healthy root produces beautiful flowers.

DC: I have seen you practising daily in the park for up to two hours at a time, but I never see you running. Why is this?

MT: I did run when I was younger, but when you are younger you try everything, just trying to be strong, but you miss something about the internal body. When I started Qigong while I was still running, I found I was exhausted – all the energy I gathered would be used up in the running. So it is with a lot of physical exercise – if we don't do it carefully, we will exhaust ourselves. Because I practise a lot every day I build up a lot of energy. If you have the balance, and understand the soft and the hard, you won't get exhausted.

DC: Have you used swimming?

MT: Swimming is fine, swimming slowly especially, but after swimming I personally suggest that you do some meditation. In fact after all practice, meditation helps recover energy and repair damage.

DC: Meditation is an interesting aspect. There are a number of doctors who advocate meditation for health, and many treatment centres use it in their practices. Would you like to comment on how people can best employ the various methods of meditation for health?

MT: There are quite a few kinds of meditation. Some meditation involves just putting the hands on the dantien at the centre – this is for gathering energy. Some meditation postures such as opening the palms releases negative energy. Others such as opening the arms is for developing stronger energy and more fitness. So meditation, no matter which position we take, is mainly the mind and body coming together. First we need to concentrate, and eventually we have to try and forget everything. Then heaven and man come together. In this sense heaven means nature. When you come to be part of nature your body will be in harmony and be able to gather lots of energy. Illnesses will automatically be discharged by nature. And a lot of the energy you need will come to you so that you become part of the universe. That is the higher level you want to reach.

DC: Many people who try to practise meditation alone have many problems, like the problems of distracting thoughts. They are not able to concentrate. How would you suggest people get around this problem if they cannot attend classes?

MT: It is possible without going to class, particularly the second method, as we can follow the book to study, but the Qigong Institute also has videos and cassettes to help people to learn. But the main reason people have difficulty concentrating is that they want to settle the body down too fast. For example, if you have a question in your mind you want to sort out, meditation can help to solve this problem. Some people can do it but a lot of people can't do it, because when the mind is so active, you expect to settle down straight away. You can't. I would suggest: follow the book, do the self massage, do some movement, then meditate. You will get a good result. If you try to do meditation straight away, you can't. It is like hot tea – how can you drink it without cooling it down?

DC: The methods shown in the book are mainly sitting and standing, although there are lying down methods of meditation.

MT: Yes, but it doesn't matter – any posture we choose is OK, standing, sitting or lying. In the beginning we need to find a method for meditation at the centre. At the centre means our dantien located below the navel, inside the body. This is the centre of gravity, and it means you choose the right posture. To find it, keep your legs equally balanced, and allow your body to settle down at the centre, where you feel comfortable and relaxed. Some people can even stand on one leg, or with their back leaning forward. If you feel heavy, it means the centre is not at the centre. So if you want to do meditation longer in the right position, keep the centre at the centre.

DC: Many people have visited the East or seen people practising Tai Chi and early morning exercises on television. How would you describe the difference between these two apparently similar exercises?

MT: There are lots of similarities, but if you study both of them, you will find a difference. I would say Tai Chi traditionally was a martial art. Even now it is still a martial art. Qigong just concentrates on the health benefits. When you practise Tai Chi, you move slowly also to gain health benefit. Modern styles of Tai Chi emphasise health and this is how Western people view it. If you look back at the people practising Tai Chi in China, you will see they move a little bit faster. But in the West there is an image of Tai Chi as a slow movement, implying it is for health only. On the one hand Tai Chi is for health, but on the other it is for self defence, i.e. the martial arts. Qigong practice is mainly based on health. Just look at one difference we see: in Tai Chi we never bend over. In Qigong we do anything – slapping, jumping, shaking sometimes with eyes closed, but Tai Chi doesn't do that. You could say Tai Chi was the first Chinese health exercise – especially in the '60s, '70s and '80s. People saw the slow movement and began to love it, because they want to move beautifully.

DC: Earlier you spoke of trying to understand Qigong. We have to know the principles behind it. Can you give the reader some indications towards these?

MT: The principle of Qigong is 'to be natural': able to do anything, practise any method. But for most people, it is very hard to be natural. For the Chinese, Taoism and Buddhism always mention emptiness or nothing. Nothing means keeping your mind empty. When your mind is empty, you are free of distracting thought, your body is relaxed and your mind can be natural. So if you have any problem and if you forget it, the answer will come automatically. Be natural, empty your mind, become nothing, relax.

DC: So what you are saying is that the state of nothingness is clarity.

MT: Yes, when you are clear you can be yourself. Don't carry anything with you in meditation, take it easy, relax, be happy.

DC: So in the state of the practice of Qigong, it is very important to employ this state of mind, to achieve the most benefit.

MT: If you want to empty the mind too much, it won't happen. So take it easy, it will come. Relax, it will come. To help us reach this state of an empty mind, what should we do? Concentrate the mind on the dantien or do something before we do nothing. For example, if you get angry and are told to calm down, it is impossible. Go out, have a walk, come back and you'll have calmed down. The walking is the 'something' for us to do to get rid of the excesses of energy in order to come back to nothing. So we would say that because we want to be nothing, so we need the something to help and something is the mother of everything and everything is the root of something.

DC: So whereas we can think of ten thousand things, you are advocating that we think of one thing for release from the 9,999 others and then eventually let go of the one thing. That is the way to achieve the right state.

MT: Yes, when you go home, you can take off your clothes. If you go out to see people, then you need to wear the clothes, when you go home. You can be empty, relax.

DC: The five element theory of Chinese medicine pervades all systems. Can you explain its relationship to Qigong practice?

MT: Five elements are not only used in Qigong – it is in all the Chinese methods. Chinese people use the five elements, for example, in philosophy, martial arts, acupuncture, medicines, food, arts; it permeates all of Chinese culture. The five elements maintain the systems of any subject: we have the wood, the fire, we have the earth, metal and water. You can see them anywhere – in your house, in the countryside, even in a modern office – although their presentation may be a little bit different, but still you can find out that they come from the five elements. The elements control each other and help each other. For example, wood can aid a fire and the fire nourishes the earth and in the earth you can find metal, and metal can be corroded by water. Water then goes up the tree, so they help each other cyclically. On the other hand, they also control each other – for example metal cuts wood and wood takes its nutrition from the earth and the earth stops the water and water puts out fire. Then fire melts the metal. Helping each other, controlling each other – you can see the positive side and you can see the negative side – to balance the whole system.

In our bodies, within Chinese medicine, we have to learn the five elements. When we refer to the liver we are saying wood – they connect together, because the liver is related to our eye like wood and when you have a liver problem, you will see the face turn a little green like wood. Fire relates to the heart – so if you have a heart attack, your face will turn red, and in the case of the spleen, this relates to the earth. When your face goes yellow nor dark brown, it is because the spleen is having problems. Metal, signified by the white colour, relates to the lungs. If you have asthma, you normally have a pale white face. Next, the kidney – it is related to water. Chinese water is symbolically a dark colour or black, so people with a kidney problem usually have low energy, and are very tired, very weak. You see the forehead and the face turn very dark and sometimes just before death the face goes even darker.

Naturally with Qigong practice we don't have to understand everything about them – we just need to understand the principle. So if you have a problem with one of the organs, for example you have a heart attack, it will cause a problem with your spleen, because of fire helping the earth. On the other hand, it will cause the kidney to have a problem, because the kidney controls the fire, so the kidney would be too strong. So they lose the balance – one organ loses the balance and causes problems to other organs. How can we do Qigong to balance a problem? When the body comes to a very natural state, as I mentioned before – a 'nothing'. By bringing your body to an empty state, then your body will automatically move because your external body lets go, like Yin and Yang, and the internal body then becomes stronger. When the internal Qi becomes stronger, then the body will start to move and energy will run all over the body strongly through the acupuncture channels and the site of the problem will be stimulated and the Qi will nourish that area. At that moment your body will move naturally, and like a deer your arms will lift up. And when you have a heart problem, your hands will extend like a bird, so that the energy will nourish the heart. When you have a problem with your stomach, your hand will automatically rub the stomach; slapping or scratching your arms and legs, stimulating the channel because of the spleen – that is the monkey. If you have asthma or breathing problems, your arms will push forward and the fingers will close together very strongly like claws – the tiger. When you have a back problem, a low energy problem, a kidney problem, your body will automatically bend forward like a bear to nourish the kidney. So each of the five elements has a different movement when you let go.

When you let go, the energy will direct you how to do it, as this form of Qigong is spontaneous. It is one of the very popular exercises in China, although some people misunderstand the spontaneity. If you understand it you won't have any problem with practice. Like all the children and animals, you won't need a doctor to heal the body. You can move your body to balance the energy all the time. That is the way Qigong uses the five elements. On the other hand, some people don't use spontaneous movements – they use the animal's movement. Some will move like a deer to nourish the liver, some imitate a bird to relate to the heart, some like a monkey for the spleen, some will move like a tiger for the lung, and some will move like a bear for the kidney – we call this five animal play. So there are many different styles employing the five elements – it's common to use the wood, fire, earth, metal and water to practise. Some people will use the timing, position and direction to relate to different organs. It's basically simple but at higher levels it becomes more complex. It's all step by step.

DC: In the first part of the book are some of the various postures for relaxation and meditation. Many people feel, I am sure, that they would like to practise meditation but they find great difficulty in being able to relax.

MT: The main problem is that people have no experience at relaxing. Everybody will find it difficult, everybody. With gentle steady practice, it eventually becomes easier to handle.

DC: You have made a study of the Wild Goose method known as Dayan Qigong, which is becoming very popular. Could you explain how you came across the Wild Goose and why you believe it to be so beneficial for people as an exercise?

MT: At first I didn't consider the Wild Goose Qigong to be special and concentrated on stronger exercises, for example martial arts and body strengthening exercises. Then I came across the Wild Goose and found it really good. So far, even after many years, I still practise the Wild Goose because the sequence is so perfect and relates to a lot of channels in acupuncture. Every time, when I finish, I feel really good and energised. Since I made a deeper study and practised regularly I realised how these exercises relate to different organs, channels and acupuncture points. The benefits of the Wild Goose are really amazing. With the Wild Goose you move beautifully and learn a lot of healing techniques – how to heal yourself with the energy and learn a lot of acupuncture points, how to get the balance with your body, and not just how to move slowly but to follow your own speed. You benefit because it is a sequence of movements. A lot of Qigong in comparison, for example hard Qigong, is not a linked series – they are single movements. When you practise, you need to remind yourself that you are going to practise these exercises, and they are a little bit harder. With Wild Goose you can just enjoy – when you do it you can enjoy the movement, enjoy the fun.

DC: Is the Wild Goose taught in China in the hospitals, in places where people are ill, or is it just for people to improve their health?
MT: Recently Yang Mei Jun celebrated her 98th birthday. She is still teaching and working in hospitals and can still read without spectacles. She is truly remarkable. Many different types of Qigong have been used in China. Some of the Wild Goose movements are used for specific illnesses, but mainly people practise outside hospital. In hospital, most of the Qigong they use is quite simple – relaxation, meditation – and not as complicated as the Wild Goose. And the Wild Goose methods chosen for treatment in some of the hospitals is sometimes only a single movement.

DC: I'm sure some readers may have come across reference to Qigong within the martial arts. What is the connection?
MT: Martial arts training can be hard work, therefore anyone practising martial arts must have more energy than the average person. Some techniques may be exhausting and sometimes injuries can occur, which is why Qigong should be practised along with regular training. There is a saying in Chinese martial arts that 'without internal training all martial arts training comes to nought'. How sad for people to practise the martial arts through their life and not to enjoy the supplementary benefits that accrue through internal practice. There are some methods of Qigong that develop exceptional strength in the body, but to practise such exercises requires a certain level of strength anyway.

Internal training helps repair and strengthen the body. Let me give you a simple example, take press-ups. . . . If you are strong then doing press-ups will increase your strength and fitness. If you're of a weak disposition then you would find them exhausting and of little benefit; people should understand their condition and act accordingly.

Traditionally in China, the martial arts have been long involved in the healing process, many skilled martial artists have practised acupuncture, bone-setting, massage, herbalism and Qigong therapy. Chinese holistic therapies require a doctor/therapist to be strong and healthy. That's why most Chinese traditional doctors practise Qigong and martial arts.

QIGONG CASE HISTORIES

I have included a number of case histories which have been published in various Chinese publications. These are some of the countless thousands of statements which have been recorded by those who have benefitted from Qigong.

WEN SHENGLAN (female, 48 years old, works in the Ministry of Geology and Mineral Products).
For several years before 1966, she suffered from pain in her whole body, the cause of which was unknown. In March 1966 the symptoms became serious. She constantly cried and her moods changed suddenly. According to the diagnosis of Third Hospital of the Beijing Medicine Institute, she suffered from hysteria. A long period of treatment, using both western and traditional Chinese medicine methods, had failed to cure her. In addition, she suffered from coronary heart disease and gastritis. Her blood pressure was very high and heart-stroke occurred very often. Several times she was critically ill and was sent to the hospital for emergency treatment. Sometimes she would suddenly faint and have a weak pulse. At times she suffered from frequent irregular systole and was often extremely weak. Even in the summer time she had to wear heavy cotton-padded trousers, two pairs of woollen pyjamas and cotton-padded shoes to keep warm. People were not permitted to use fans when Wen Shenglan was in a room. She could not fan herself because her bones would ache. When she was frightened a little, her legs would feel loose and she could not walk at all.

Since 1982, Wen has been practising types of Qigong and Taijiquan. Her diseases have been gradually alleviated and her health has recovered. Hysteria has been cured, her heart stroke has not occurred for a long time, and gastritis, from which she suffered for 40 years, has also been cured. Meanwhile practising these types of Qigong and Taijiquan has cured her of some other diseases such as arthritis, pelvic inflammation, heavy constipation, and abdominal distention. Now she has become healthy and in the summer she doesn't have to wear winter clothing; moreover, she can fan herself when necessary. She said, 'In the past, I was a person who suffered from serious diseases. Qigong and Taijiquan have rescued me from the hands of the King of Hell.'

XU WENMING (male, 60 years old, driver for the Beijing Trolleybus Company).

In the past Mr Xu suffered from several diseases, including hypertension, nephritis, and piles. His blood pressure was 190/120 mm. The results of his urine test were: urinary albumin + +, white blood cells 0.3-0.5, red blood cells 0.5-1.0. He did not recover after his piles had been treated; a swelling in his anus appeared, when he suffered from excessive internal heat.

Since June 1983, Mr Xu has been practising Qigong and Taijiquan. He practises for an hour and a half each morning, and has achieved remarkable results. His blood pressure has now been reduced to 150/100 mm. Tests have also revealed that the symptoms of his nephritis have been remarkably alleviated. The results of a urine test: urinary albumin reduced to +, white blood cells − 0.1, red blood cells − 0.3. His piles and splenopathy have been completely cured. He now eats and sleeps very well and has become a brisk walker. He can work for a long time without being tired. He has not needed to see a doctor for more than one year. His temper has become better.

ZHANG SHUYUN (female, 61 years old, a cadre of Beijing Foreign Language Institute).

Zhang suffered from coronary heart disease with heart strokes and irregular systole. She also suffered from constipation. Since 1981 she has been practising Qigong and Taijiquan. The symptoms of the diseases have gradually alleviated. There has been no recurrence of heart stroke or irregular systole. She no longer suffers from constipation.

PENG WENZHANG (male, 53 years old, a secretary in Secretariat of the General Office of the Ministry of Geology and Mineral Products).

Mr Peng suffered from an amnesic syndrome. As a secretary he was to keep the minutes of meetings, but he could not remember the names of those attending; therefore, he was unable to fulfil his main task. Besides, he could not read documents, did not sleep well, and often lost his temper, which had not been characteristic of him.

Since early 1984 Mr Peng has been practising Qigong and has achieved remarkable curative results. Now Mr Peng eats and sleeps well and his memory functions well. He can now keep the minutes of a meeting, read documents, and even write articles. Meanwhile, the symptoms of puffiness, which he had suffered from, also disappeared. He has become a brisk walker, and a healthy strong man.

XIE SHANCHU (male, 74 years old. He was a businessman in Beijing and now lives at 30 Dong Yang Ma Ying Street, Western District, Beijing).
Mr Xie was very weak and walked in a doddering manner. Since 1983 he has been practising Qigong. Now Mr Xie has recovered his youthful vigour and walks like a young man.

QIAN LIANGYU (female, age 49, teacher at the middle school attached to the People's University).
Began to suffer from hypertension in 1971. Medical treatment proved to be of no avail and her condition went from bad to worse until her blood pressure rose to 220/130 mmHg in 1978. Meanwhile, she fell victim to insomnia and could sleep no more than three or four hours every night even though she always took a sedative before going to bed. Prolonged illness reduced her to agony and despair.

   After going in for Qigong, she could get along without taking medicine. Within a month her sleep had improved remarkably: every day she went to bed after 9.30 pm and did not wake up until 5:30 the next morning. By the end of another month her blood pressure had dropped to a stable level of 150/90 mmHg. Her mental attitude had also greatly improved.

JIANG HUA (female, 54, worker at Beijing No. 798 Plant).
Suffered from chronic hepatitis for over 20 years. Troubled by insomnia as well. Hb:6g. Ate only 2-3 *liang*, or 100-150 g., of staple food a day. Forced to retire because of illness.

   After a few weeks of Qigong practice, she felt much better and could consume 100-150 g. of staple food *per meal*. Her sleep had also improved.

   Hb was increased to 9 g. within a month and 12.7g. within three months. Liver function was restored to normal in four months.

SHAO XIU-E (female, 51, administrative cadre at the Beijing Boiler Plant).
Case history:
(1) PYELONEPHRITIS – RBC found in urine; edema.

(2) SEQUELAE OF BRAIN THROMBUS – numbness in the limbs.

   After three months of Qigong exercise, she felt stronger and light of foot. Results in repeated routine urine tests were normal. Numbness in limbs and edema had disappeared. Waist measurement had decreased from 86 cm to 80 cm.

FAN JINGZHONG (male, 49, administrator at the No. 502 Research Institute of the Ministry of Astronautics Industry).

Case history:
(1) HEART DISEASE – arrhythmia.

(2) RHEUMATOID DISEASE – lumbago which made movement difficult. Back of hands was covered with large, black flecks attributable to old age.

After two months of Qigong practice, the heart problem was noticeably alleviated and the patient was able to exercise self-control when he did not feel well. For two years now there has been no relapse of the disease. Lumbago has also become much less intense. The patient can now move about easily and can even bend his waist. The flecks on his hands have become lighter in colour and less protruding than before.

XIE HUANZHANG (male, 64, professor at Beijing Industrial College).
Has been suffering from hypertension for 11 years, his blood pressure reaching 200/120 mmHG at one time. Also troubled by constipation.

Blood pressure dropped to a stable level of 140/70 mmHg after two months' Qigong practice, during which time no medicine was taken. Constipation was also assuaged.

WANG SHANGRUI (male, 74, retired worker).
Suffered from lumbago for many years. After two months' Qigong practice, his appetite has increased, he can sleep very well and no longer feels any pain in the lumbar region. His eyesight and hearing have also markedly improved. He can now read without wearing glasses and can hear the clicking sound of a watch placed behind his ears. He feels more energetic than ever.

THE QIGONG INSTITUTE

Founded in 1988, the Institute offers learning courses and treatment therapy for those wishing to benefit from these unique health skills that form part of the central theory of Traditional Chinese Medicine.

All enquiries:
Qigong Institute,
18, Swan Street,
Manchester M4 5JN
England
. . . Tel: 061 832 8204

Also available from the above address: *Tai Chi* by Danny Connor, £9.99